Eddie Fisher

What do project managers really do? Do they push their projects and lead their people?

GRIN Verlag

Bibliografische Information der Deutschen Nationalbibliothek:

Die Deutsche Bibliothek verzeichnet diese Publikation in der Deutschen National-
bibliografie; detaillierte bibliografische Daten sind im Internet über http://dnb.d-
nb.de/ abrufbar.

Imprint:

Copyright © 2007 GRIN Verlag GmbH
Druck und Bindung: Books on Demand GmbH, Norderstedt Germany
ISBN: 978-3-656-20418-3

This book at GRIN:

http://www.grin.com/en/e-book/112185/what-do-project-managers-really-do-do-
they-push-their-projects-and-lead

GRIN - Your knowledge has value

Der GRIN Verlag publiziert seit 1998 wissenschaftliche Arbeiten von Studenten, Hochschullehrern und anderen Akademikern als eBook und gedrucktes Buch. Die Verlagswebsite www.grin.com ist die ideale Plattform zur Veröffentlichung von Hausarbeiten, Abschlussarbeiten, wissenschaftlichen Aufsätzen, Dissertationen und Fachbüchern.

Visit us on the internet:

http://www.grin.com/

http://www.facebook.com/grincom

http://www.twitter.com/grin_com

"What Do Project Managers Really Do? Do They Push Their Projects And Lead Their People?"

Author: Dr Eddie Fisher

Presented at the PM Days '07 Projects & Management: From 9-5? Conference, Vienna, 7-8 May 2007

Abstract

The working day of project managers has changed. Today's working environments place higher demands on project managers. More is expected in less time, with fewer people and to higher quality standards. Project Managers need to push their teams and themselves harder to achieve the expected results. They need to adopt new or improved working with people competences and associated behaviours to be successful in their endeavours.

I will discuss what project managers typically do, what they need to do in future and how they can achieve the desired results.

1   Introduction

Project Management has been around for a long time. Morris (1994, p.1) considers that ' Managing projects is one of the oldest and most respected accomplishments of mankind. We stand in awe of the pyramids, the architects of ancient sites, the masons and craftsmen of great cathedrals and mosques, of the might and labour behind the Great Wall of China and other wonders of the world'. Gareis (2005) suggests that ' In the project-oriented society projects and programmes are becoming more important not only in profit and non-profit organizations, but also in new areas of application, such as in small communities, associations, schools and even in families'. The changes in working environments and the new business expectations have had a major impact on project managers. According to Gareis and Huemann (2003) project managers are now expected to deliver more in less time, to higher quality standards and with fewer resources. It appears that the working day of projects managers, therefore, has changed in line with these developments.

I will consider in the next Section what the typical working day of a project manager looked like in the past, what it is today and how we can make some assumptions what it could or should look like in future. I will discuss in Section 3 whether project managers push their projects hard enough. I will suggest in Section 4 what managing people competences and behaviours project managers should adopt and the likely effect this could have on their working day, and their effectiveness. I will present the conclusions drawn from the discussions in Section 5.

2 The Working Day of the Project Manager

2.1 The Past

Prior to the 1990s, project management was perhaps not given the importance it deserved. It appears that this was due to the prevailing working practices and environments at that time such as hierarchical ways of working rather than matrix working (Turner,1993; Gareis,1990). It appears that this affected what project managers did during their normal working day and how they managed their projects. It is probably true to say that project managers in those days worked standard working hours such as 9 to 5, depending on which country they worked in. They concentrated more on the tasks than the people they worked with. Much of their time was spent on planning the activities of their projects, setting up project plans and putting together project schedules. The primary focus was on tools and techniques such as CPA and PERT. Project managers directed their people more rather than engage them more in the project through consultation. Management by fear was quite common at that time.

Project managers spent much of their time to interpret the requirements of key stakeholders. This was due to the fact that they were often given insufficient details of what they were expected to deliver, often lacking clarity on whether time, cost or quality was more important. So it was up to the project manager to develop what he thought was expected and then deliver the project accordingly. They probably spent a lot of their time dealing with and managing change requests. These were frequent due to the nature of the working practices such as hierarchical management structures where project managers were simply told ' to get on with it'. The changes in working environments and practices that started during the early 1990s had a major impact on the working day of project managers. I will discuss this in the next Section.

2.2 The Present

Gareis (2005) considers that the perception of projects as temporary organizations dramatically increases the importance of project management. He acknowledges that projects with different objectives (such as contracting projects, offer projects, marketing projects, organizational projects and personnel development projects, etc.) in all branches of industry, in the public sector and in non-profit organizations, could increase an organization's efficiency and chances of survival. In addition to projects of high complexity, small projects and projects of medium complexity increase in importance.

The typical working day of today's project managers changed as a direct result of these developments. Many projects are now truly global projects. Generally, project managers work longer hours and often cross different time zones, meaning very early or very late conference calls or video link-ups. Senior Management expects more flexibility from their project managers.

So what do today's project managers typically do during their working days? Recent research (Fisher, 2006; Huemann, 2002; Blackburn, 2001 and Crawford, 2000) suggests that a shift in focus and emphasis has developed recently. Project managers spend much more of their time on the people side than on tools and techniques. It appears that effective communications is a key activity that can take up to 60% or more of a project manager's time. This includes spending time with the team, suppliers, stakeholders, peers, Senior Management and individuals to communicate, for example, the progress of the project, seek guidance or direction and resolve issues associated with the project. Forms of communication are meetings, presentations, phone calls, E-mails and video/audio conference links. Project managers place high levels of priority on these activities. If communications break down, the project is doomed to fail.

Project managers spend more time on managing processes such as Prince 2, Six Sigma, Primavera and internal project management methodologies. This includes project health checks and audits to ensure that project team members comply with these. Other regular tasks include:

Finance: Prepare the business case, manage Earned Value Analysis, control the budget and liaise closely with the Finance Department

Team Building: Build the project team, coach team members, leading the team and managing people issues

Documentation: Set up the project files, prepare templates, writing of reports, minutes of meetings, prepare the project plan and schedule and manage E-mails

In addition, other daily tasks include making appropriate decisions (sometimes ad hoc), negotiating for project resources, influencing key stakeholders and senior management regarding the direction of the project.

Based on her research on what project managers do, Blackburn (2001) suggests that project managers spend a considerable amount of their time on:

1. Listening a lot to users to understand their problems
2. Consider and propose new working processes and agree these with the users
3. Meeting with people 'on their ground' to resolve issues
4. Building relationships with involved parties
5. Influencing the people involved in the project
6. Managing negative feedback and share with team as appropriate
7. Building networks of people, inside and outside of the organisation
8. Planning and organising
9. Managing issues and risks and dependencies
10. Carrying out change control investigations, leading to Yes/No decisions rechanges that affect the project plan
11. Monitoring of progress

Morris, Jamieson and Shepherd (2006) consider what project managers actually do depends on, of course, on the type of projects they manage within their respective industries. For example, construction projects will often have EVA measures in place to check the financial performance of the project, whereas there will be less a requirement for EVA in drug testing projects. They consider that project managers engage in around 50 or so topics at any one time, based on the APM Body of Knowledge (2006) edition. As considered earlier, this does not mean that project managers work on each topic on every project. Some of the key areas for each project are:

- Develop project success criteria
- Risk and issue management
- Resource Management
- Project documentation such as Definition, Plan, Schedule and Communications Plan
- Business case
- Financial controls such as EVA
- Design and development
- Implementation
- Auditing/Health checks and quality management
- Building and leading the team
- Managing conflict
- Negotiating with all parties
- Stakeholder management

Looking at what Turner (2003) considers to be specific team competences of the project team, it gives some indications what project managers do or need to do during their working day:

- Co-ordinate the project team
- Report the project to the relevant environments
- Formulate the project assignment
- Build the team
- Agree project objectives with the team members
- Develop project plans
- Set up the project organisation
- Issue and Risk management
- Relationship development: inside and outside of organisations
- Resource management
- Quality management
- Control management
- Set up appropriate communications plan
- Ensure status reports are delivered and challenged
- Closing down of projects

Gareis (2005, p.79) defines the role of the project manager as 'the central integration role in the project. The project manager is the contact person for all members of the project organisation and the representatives of the relevant project environments. The project manager "drives" the project, is interested in the progress of the work and in the successful close-down of the project'. He suggests that project managers typically carry out the following activities during their working day:

- Design the project management process
- Co-ordinate all project management activities
- Control and close down the project
- Set up the communications plan
- Ensure project management methodology is used
- Ensure IT and Telecoms tools are used
- Develop and adapt project management documentation
- Realise project interests
- Lead the team
- Design the project organisation
- Agree project objectives with team
- Develop the project plan
- Identify and manage project risks
- Manage the project resources
- Ensure status reports are produced and their content is challenged

2.3   The Future

The working day of project managers has changed dramatically over the years. Gone are the days of 9 to 5 working. Many projects are truly global, stretching across time zones and cultural boundaries. The realisation of projects as temporary organisations has contributed to the increasing importance many companies place on project management. This had a major impact on the working environment and working practices of organisations, and thus project managers. They need to spend more time to manage the people side effectively. For example, they need to invest some of their time to empower project team members more so they can delegate more tasks, thus releasing more time they need to spend on planning their own work load more effectively.

Stakeholder analysis seems to be an increasingly important task for project managers as part of their daily routines. They need to invest regular time in this to not only keep key stakeholders informed of progress but also to secure their ongoing support for the project, including financial support and sign offs. Regular contacts are essential for this to work well. Project managers need to adopt and apply new or improved managing people competences, as suggested by research carried out by Fisher (2006). By managing people better in their projects, project managers will be able to plan their time better and achieve superior results.

It is perhaps inappropriate to put a time limit on the typical working day of project managers. Projects are about managing change, and as such, project managers need to spend whatever time it takes to deliver their projects successfully. The notion of 9 to 5 carries an inherent limitation. International projects do not run 9 to 5-they operate 24/7. Project managers who spend a considerable amount of their time to manage the people in their projects well, are more likely to deliver their projects successfully. It appears that when the people side is managed well, the effective application of tools and techniques often follows as a matter of course. Fisher (2006) who carried out some research recently in the area of effective management of people in projects, suggests that project managers need to adopt new or improved managing people competences and associated behaviours to manage people in projects more effectively. This will be discussed in more detail in Section 4.

3 The Need to Push Harder

Gareis (2005) suggests that ' The social environments of companies can be seen as being increasingly complex. Due to the globalisation of markets, new technological developments, new co-operative relationships with customers and suppliers as well as changing values in society, the complexity in the environment is increasing'. Companies such as O2, Orange and Vodafone are putting more pressure on their project managers to deliver products and services, for example, much quicker into the market. It seems that the obvious solution is for project managers to push their team members harder to meet company expectations. Some project managers do this through the application of appropriate incentive schemes such as performance-related bonus, gifts, ad hoc rewards and taking teams out for a meal/drinks at various phases of the project. Others invest money and time in developing team members more through appropriate training. Either approach does contribute somewhat towards keeping people motivated. When this happens for the right reasons, it is more likely that people can be pushed harder by the project manager to deliver more.

Experienced project managers will know when they can push their people no further. This is sometimes reflected in people's behaviour or expressed through their opinions during discussions. For example, a previously totally committed team member may start to express negative thoughts towards the project or the project manager. This could be a clear indication that the project manager is pushing too hard. Some project managers have personal reasons for pushing their teams very hard. These can be based on the ambitious attitude of the project manager who wishes to do well and demonstrate to his seniors that he can do even more. This explains why some project managers distance themselves from the team members. They create a certain power distance so they can be very firm and direct with the people they manage. Pushing hard thus becomes part of their daily routine to achieve their personal goals.

Project managers can and should push hard once they have been 'creating the conditions for motivating the members of the project organization (Gareis, 2005 and Stummer, M., 2005). They need to lead and guide their team members to deliver more in less time and with fewer resources. To achieve this, they need to gain commitment from their team members, not just compliance. Compliance is short-lived and does not bring any real long-term commitment to the project. Effective project managers clearly understand the limits of pushing hard. They will not push people continuously over the limit but consider to bring in additional resources to manage the shortfalls effectively. This will foster a work environment that supports the team members. Short-term hard pushes are perfectly acceptable in such working environments, for example, to deal with unforeseen issues or sudden changes in the project. When pushing people hard, effective project managers use language such as ' We will succeed' and ' We will go forward'.

4 New/Improved People Competences and Associated Behaviours for Project Managers

The typical working day of project managers is made up of interacting with many people, both internal and external to the project, particularly with key stakeholders, peers, suppliers, and of course, the project team members. Project managers need to have appropriate managing people competences and associated behaviours to cope with the changes in working environments and practices discussed earlier. The outcomes of the working day of project managers are affected by how they manage the people in their projects. Fisher (2006) carried out some research and suggested some new and improved competences and associated behaviours for working with people, for project managers. His research was based on a phenomenological research paradigm, with a constructivist interpretivist approach that allowed him to get close to the subject matter. The competences and associated behaviours are:

1 Competence: Understanding Behavioural Characteristics

Be genuine and open and honest with others. Show openly that you believe in your team members' abilities. Show an open and authentic concern for others that is based on true feelings and not on invented ones. Develop an understanding of the relationship between behaviours and feelings and how you can make this work for you in your teams. Adopt a repertoire of behaviours so you can deal with people in different situations and circumstances. Develop behaviours such as managing anger, asking open questions and being aware of the feelings of others. Apply only behaviours that come natural to you and not forced ones. Apply appropriate behaviours regularly so they become natural to you and the people you are dealing with.

2 Competence: Leading Others

This refers to the intention for you to take a role as leader of a team or other group. Although it implies a desire to lead others and so can be manifested in the form of a formal authority and responsibility, effective team leadership also requires you to know when not to act authoritatively if you wish to get the best out of your team. Maintain a high level of morale by leading by example. Show being motivated to lead innovation. Lead more by example and adopt a leadership style that is appropriate to the situation, for example, situational, transitional, visionary or charismatic. Ensure that your team members comply with your wishes. Apply directive, firm or demanding behaviours according to the attitudes and behaviours of your team members. Adapt your leadership behaviours to manage the different attitudes and behaviours of temporary staff such as contract project managers or support staff appropriately as compared to full time members of staff who, it appears, have a different attitude towards the company they work for and the people they work with (different goals and objectives).

3 Competence: Influencing Others

Feel at home in unfamiliar territories and engage in related activities quickly. Convince, influence or impress others in order to support their agenda, or the desire to have a specific impact or effect on others. Influence others by selling them the benefit, for example, why they should change so they can see the benefit and make the appropriate changes to their behaviour or attitude. Share with others what it feels like to work in a highly successful team so they adopt the behaviours that are associated with success. Influence team members to unblock the values and beliefs people have to help them develop better. Share with others what it feels like to work in a highly-valued team. Discuss with team members the characteristics that are sometimes helpful and sometimes hindering to help others to stop thinking small, and starting to expand their horizons. Understand the relationship between how well managers can influence others and the level of trust that exists between them. Investigate work or people situations first and then adapt your own behaviours according to the situation. Understand which buttons to push in people to generate certain responses so you can genuinely influence others more effectively.

4 Competence: Authentizotic Behaviour

Show open concern for others. Accept people for what they are and do not try to force them to change. Empower people by delegating tasks to them and ask them to take on board more responsibilities. Develop an understanding of what makes the other person tick and what is important to that person. Show genuine concerns and feelings for the needs of others. Make people feel good about work, themselves, others and the project itself. Help people to understand more about their strengths and weaknesses and limitations, and prevent them from engaging in self-destructing activities. Make people feel special and valued, by giving compliments, genuinely and from the heart.

Tune into the emotional needs of people, instil a sense of belonging, pride and confidence in everything they do and show openly empathy and support for your team members. Give open and honest feedback on performance to others so that these can improve their performance in future.

5 Competence: Conflict Management

Establish the root causes of the conflict by talking to others openly and honestly to find out. Concentrate on the work issues and do not get personal. Show loyalty, integrity, trust, help and support when dealing with conflicts. Be tolerant and prepared to compromise. Create environments of rational and objective exchange of information. Consider accepting conflicts for what they are and manage these accordingly. Observe behaviours of team members to sense early when conflicts begin to develop and then take corrective actions to resolve these. Concentrate on the emotional side of any conflict and take the sting out before this escalates into something much bigger .Be persuasive, negotiate realistically and take the lead during the influencing process. Create a kind of war room for managing conflicts (neutral ground) and bring together all parties involved in the conflict to resolve it more effectively in this type of forum. Apply different approaches to managing conflict, depending on whether they you are dealing with people, testing or implementation conflicts (technical and human conflicts).

6 Competence: Cultural Awareness

Develop, display and apply an awareness of the cultural differences of team members. Show an understanding and knowledge of the values and beliefs of other cultures. Adapt some of other people's own home country behaviours appropriate to the situation when managing people from diverse cultures. Adopt cultural awareness behaviours to manage people in their projects effectively. Show an open optimism about cultural differences and show views that confirm that you see cultural diversity as an enhancement to your own values and beliefs. Show an understanding of what the various trends, sequences and traditions are for people you work with. Understand that some people from different cultures may have one set of values at work but another set at home. Make sure that you do not bring the home culture to the foreign culture, without due consideration how one might impact on the other. Understand that different companies have different company cultures, for example, how work is done within the company or how their employees are expected to perform or behave. Remove language barriers by being clear, talking slowly and pronouncing words well, and paraphrasing statements to ensure your message sent equals the other person's message received.

Project managers who apply these are more likely to manage the people in their projects effectively. Their working day will be affected, too. For example, understanding why people behave in certain ways such as being open and genuine with people and understanding what is important to others, means that project managers can delegate more work and empower team members to take on more responsibilities. Project managers can then concentrate more on work that is appropriate for them to do, such as keeping a close rapport with key stakeholders, align the project to the strategy or to seek new business opportunities for future projects.

5   Conclusions

The typical working day of project managers has changed considerably. Influenced by changes in working environments and practices, project managers do no longer work a standard 9 to 5 day. They are put under increasing pressure by their companies and/or senior management to deliver more in less time and with fewer resources. They spend more of their time on following established processes such as Prince 2 and Six Sigma, and other project management tools, techniques and methodologies. Many companies now operate globally across different time zones. The working day of project managers often starts very early and finishes very late, for example, to participate in audio or video conference links.

There is a gap between the changes in working environments and practices and the managing people competences and associated behaviours project managers need to adopt to manage people more effectively. People are more important than tools and techniques. Project managers need to push harder to get more out of their people. This will put them back in control of their working days so they can concentrate more on their own work load and make more effective use of their time. Applying the suggested new or improved managing people competences and associated behaviours considered by recent research will put project managers back in the driving seat and enable them to manage the people in their projects more effectively.

References

Blackburn, S.(2001).*Understanding Project Managers At Work,* Henley Management College/Brunel University, DBA Thesis

Crawford, L.H.(2000).*Project Management Competence: The Value Of Standards,* A thesis submitted for the degree of Doctor of Business Administration, Henley Management College/Brunel University, United Kingdom

Fisher, E.J.P. (2006).*An empirical investigation to develop a new competence model for working with people and associated behaviours for project managers,* Open University, United Kingdom, Ph.D. Thesis

Gareis, R.(ed.,1990)*The Handbook of Management by Projects,* Manz

Gareis, R. (2005).*Happy Projects!,* Manz Verlag, Vienna

Gareis, R. and Huemann, M. (2003).*Project Management competences in the project-oriented organization,* in J.R. Turner (ed.) *People in Project Management,* Gower

Gareis, R. (2005, in co-operation with Stummer, M.).*Happy Projects!,* Manz Verlag, Vienna

Huemann, M.(2002).*Individuelle Projektmanagement-Kompetenzen in Projektorientierten Unternehmen,* University for Economics and Management, Vienna, Ph.D. Thesis

Morris, P.W.G.(1994).*The management of projects,* 1st Edition, London: Thomas Telford

Morris, P.W.G.;Jamieson, A. and Shepherd, M.M. (2006).*Research updating the APM Body of Knowledge 4th edition,* International Journal of Project Management, 24, 6, pages 461-473

Turner, J.R.(2003).*People in Project Management,* Gower Publishing Limited

Turner, J.R.(1993).*The Handbook of Project-Based Management, McGraw-Hill Publishing Company*